The Arco Book of Useful Knots

The Arco Book of
Useful Knots

John Russell

Arco Publishing, Inc.
New York

© John Russell 1981

This edition published by Arco Publishing, Inc.,
219 Park Avenue South, N.Y. 10003

First published in Great Britain in 1981
by Ward Lock Limited, 47 Marylebone Lane,
London W1M 6AX, a Pentos Company.

Designed by Heather Sherratt

Jacket photograph by John Watney

Text filmset in Times
by M & R Computerised Typesetting Ltd, Grimsby
Printed in Hong Kong

Library of Congress Catalog Card Number 81-10977
ISBN 0-668-05372-0

Contents

'There is less in this than meets the eye'

Tallulah Bankhead

On using this book

This book is about working knots, those that you tie where and when you want them, using no tools but your hands, and cast off again when their work is done. It does not touch upon that great category of permanent knots which includes all multi-strand knots such as splices, coverings, buttons, mats, braids (which the sailor calls sennits), all the purely decorative knots, and extends into net and rug making, crochet and knitting. You could call those 'workshop knots' because they are made at leisure and never dismantled, and because their construction often involves the preparation of materials, the use of tools and sometimes even of drawings. The study of them is a huge subject that needs, not only much space, but an understanding of the elements of knot making that is best attained through familiarity with the humbler and simpler working knots.

Everyone has always needed knots, but none has depended on them so completely as the seaman, nor made and used them under such hostile and demanding conditions. Consequently, the seaman's knots are the most numerous and versatile, and his methods of tying them meet exigencies of which few landsmen are aware: his repertoire of knots includes something to suit every conceivable purpose, and his techniques set forth the logic of knot construction and knot behaviour with a clarity that no student of the subject can afford to miss.

The knots I have chosen to describe are all practical and useful, and most of them are well-known and widely used; but they are also there because of the incidental light which they cast on the subject as a whole, and in some instances so that we can re-examine the limitations of a few that are habitually misused.

After much thought and some experiment I decided against trying to tinker with the sailor's language. Like the knots themselves, nautical terminology has been shaped by urgent need, in this instance to communicate swiftly and unambiguously. Any attempt to translate the unfamiliar words into 'plain English' without losing precision, demands much more effort from the reader than that he should become familiar with a dozen words and their meanings. The explanation of the anatomy of knots includes the nautical terms and there is a glossary as well.

The book is designed to be read 'rope in hand' so that the operations can be repeated step-by-step as you read. For this you need two pieces of rope or cord, each about one metre long. Cheap clothesline will do, but do not use anything that is either excessively stiff or limp, nor as thin as string or fishing line. If you make a mistake in tying a knot do not untie it there and then but leave it until you have got it right and then compare your efforts and see not only where you went wrong but what effect your false move had on the knot. I hope that you will not be content to follow the main road of the instructions but will experiment along the side turnings as well.

I would never have attained to a sufficient understanding of the anatomy of knots had it not been for the systematic work of the late Clifford W. Ashley whose encyclopaedic work 'The Ashley Book of Knots' has been a constant source of verification and arbiter of doubt. I am grateful to John Watney for his inexhaustible dedication and patience in taking and retaking the scores of photographs from which the illustrations were chosen, to Peter and Robert Smyth for being such co-operative models, and to my wife Joanna, and daughter-in-law Jennet for doing all the backstage chores.

Working knots

Working Knots are traditionally and conveniently divided into knots, bends and hitches according to the purposes for which they are used.

True knots are lumps, knobs or loops in a single line.
Binding knots are tied round an object or bundle of objects, usually with the ends of the encircling line.
Bends join two lines end to end.
Hitches secure a line to another object (which may include a loop or eye in another line), or to part of another line other than its end.

Some knots that are named 'bends', such as fisherman's bend and topsail halyard bend, are in fact hitches. The sailor tries to explain this by saying that he always talks of 'bending on' a sail or an anchor (the purposes for which these two knots are generally used), but he is not always consistent about this and anyway the word knot is applied loosely to the whole species.

The attributes of working knots
Simplicity
Every working knot must be capable of being tied quickly. Very often it will have to be made in the brief interval between the line being brought to the object to which it must be secured and its subjection to a strain that may prevent the knot being tied. Any delay while you rack your brains for the next move is as intolerable as that caused by a series of complicated manipulations, so the knot must be both easy to tie and to remember. The simplicity of working knots comes as a great

9

surprise to the uninstructed, whose mistakes in knot-making very often arise from their efforts to make the knot more complicated than it is.

Strength
All knots involve changing the direction of the rope's axis and the pinching or 'nipping' of one part by another. Nips and angles of very sharp radius distort and weaken rope, and although present day synthetic fibres are so strong that a rope of a size that is comfortable to handle probably has an enormous margin of strength in any domestic or sporting application, the effect of the knot has to be taken into account if this margin is reduced.

Security
Far more frequently critical than its strength is a knot's ability to stay done up. When loaded, an insecure knot may slip or it may capsize and spill, but more searching than straightforward strain is the repeated alternation between strain and relaxation that is typical of the working condition of knots that are used at sea and also those that are used to tether animals. Much depends on the material of which the rope is made: stiff and springy material is notoriously apt to open up knots even when completely at rest, while slippery stuff presents a more predictable problem. Such materials narrow the choice of knots that can be used.

However intrinsically secure a knot may be, it can be ruined if it has been carelessly formed. This has nothing to do with the way in which it is tied but in the closeness and evenness with which it has been snugged together, so that it retains its correct formation under strain. There is a knack to this which can only be developed by practice: it soon becomes automatic but the beginner has to make conscious efforts to ensure that his knots are not sloppy and unstable.

Last, but not least, of the factors affecting security is the length of the rope's ends after the knot has been made: ends that are too short, the hallmark of the ignorant, can be the starting point of an otherwise sound knot's disintegration.

In certain types of knot that have special purposes, like slipknots, security may have to be subordinated to effectiveness in their particular role. In this event the knot has to be treated as a temporary one, only replacing a more secure one shortly before it is needed.

Bends seem to pose more problems than other types of knot, and their security can be affected by differences in thickness, construction and composition of the two ropes involved. Some bends are only suitable for joining identical ropes.

Ease of adjustment

In most circumstances this is a minor consideration, but for some purposes it may be desirable to use a knot that can be adjusted without the need to cast it off and re-tie it. Control lines, lashings and tent guys commonly need this facility which is a prime feature of the rolling hitch and is present to a more limited degree in the bowline.

Ease of release

Plenty of landsmen's knots are never intended to yield to anything less than the knife, but at sea a knot that jams is an intolerable nuisance and even a danger. Exceptionally, a seaman may compromise for the sake of extra security and use a knot that draws up pretty tight so that he has to put in some strenuous work and even a tap or two with a belaying pin, but any knot that has to be opened with a spike ranks as a permanent or workshop knot. Ease of release need not necessarily be paid for in lowered security; once again the rolling hitch comes to mind as an example of a thoroughly secure knot that is outstandingly easy to let go even when under load. But for certain knots this is their primary function and they would be misused in any application in which it was not needed.

Possibility of prefabrication

Sometimes it is necessary to have a knot ready for action rather than having to tie it round something. The seaman's expression for making a knot round nothing but air is to tie it 'in hand', a term which is meaningless in relation to bends. The capability of being tied in hand is an important property in loop knots and some like the figure eight loop and bowline on a bight, cannot be tied any other way except in the most artificial and unlikely circumstances.

These qualities are present in varying proportions in every well-designed knot, and the intelligent use of knots consists of choosing the knot that has the correct blend of qualities for its purpose.

Basic anatomy and definitions

A piece of rope looks much the same from one end to the other, but it does have two ends. The one you manipulate in the formation of a knot is called the working end, and the length of rope adjacent to it the working part: both terms relate strictly to the process of knot making and have nothing to do with the load-bearing function of the rope. The other end, which in practice is often fixed, is called the standing end, and any part of the rope which is not active in the making of a knot the standing part. This is usually the load-bearing part.

Any slack part of the rope between its ends is referred to as the bight, but the word is used more specifically for a wide loop corresponding to the geographical term for a bay so open that a sailing ship can leave it whatever the wind direction, without tacking.

Elongating a bight makes a loop. This is the first of the knot-building formations (fig. 1).

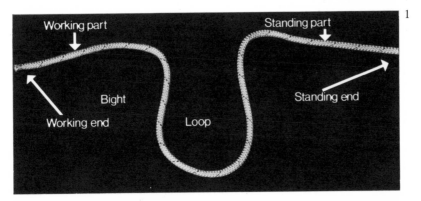

1

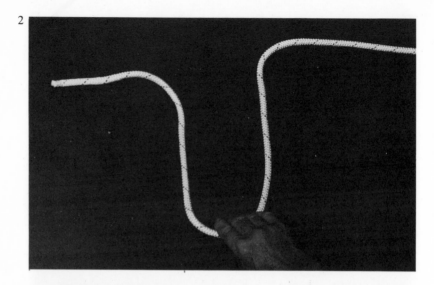

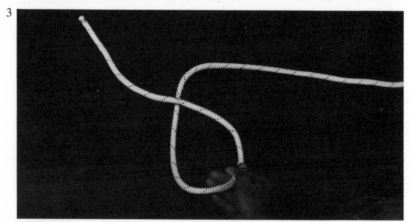

Turning the loop over so that its limbs cross, converts it into a turn (figs. 2 and 3). This is the second basic formation.

As you perform this action of converting a loop into a turn you notice that the rope to either side rotates a little on its axis as you turn the loop over. This is a common feature of all rope handling: every movement of the rope is accompanied by some degree of twisting which has to be sensed through the fingers and helped to dissipate itself along the rope so that it may take up the shape you want to put into it without stubborn resistance and the formation of annoying kinks. It is only a small step from sensing this twist to the realisation that you can make a turn, either from a loop or from a straight section of the bight simply by twisting the rope with a turn of the wrist.

If you take a turn round an object such as a rail or another rope and cross one part over the other (fig. 4) there will be a point of pressure and friction where they cross. This pressure point is called a 'nip'. Nip is the essential ingredient of any knot and its introduction here has converted the turn into a single hitch. Pause for a moment now, and feel the effect of putting a strain first on one part of the rope and then on the other, thus in effect reversing the standing and working ends.

Now let go both ends. You will find that nip disappears and the single hitch reverts to being a turn. By itself the single hitch

4

is no knot, it needs something to keep it in shape and maintain the existence of nip.

Knot making really boils down to arranging the rope in such a way that nip is preserved for as long as it is needed throughout the circumstances of its use. The formations that are used, and the order in which they are used, determine a knot's performance and the proportions in which its various characteristics appear. In practice it is all amazingly simple, most working knots consisting of at most three stages, each stage consisting of nothing more than the few basic formations we are now discovering. To take as an example once again that most secure and easily cast off knot the rolling hitch is no more than a single hitch to create nip, a turn to add frictional area and to preserve the shape of the first single hitch, and a final single hitch to prevent the idle end from undoing the knot.

This very simplicity in combining such a small number of formations should alert us to Ashley's axiom that there is no such thing as a small mistake in knot tying: a knot cannot be slightly wrong, it is either right or it is the wrong knot, or no knot at all.

We could just as easily have made the single hitch round its own standing part (fig. 5) with the loop so formed round

5

another object. This is a half hitch, and although the single hitch and half hitch are commonly referred to by this same term they are separate and distinct formations.

Like the other basic formations the half hitch by itself is of little use as a knot: when tightened it jams under strain, and when not tightened it slips and comes undone. Nevertheless it is widely used in the construction of many knots and it has some interesting and important characteristics.

If you tie a half hitch like that in fig. 5 and then straighten out the working part of the line (the part which is single hitched round the other) the hitch will be cast into the opposite part (figs. 6 and 7). This alteration of the form of a knot without adding or subtracting anything is called 'capsizing': it is sometimes induced deliberately in making a knot but is more usually a possibility that has to be guarded against.

6

7

8

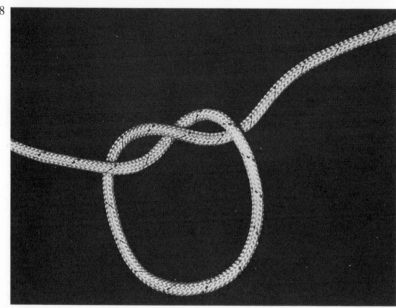

Going back now to the turn, let us see how else it can be developed. The working end can be taken across the standing part and stuck through the turn from the opposite side (fig. 8). If the knot so formed is drawn tight to make a lump in the rope we have the overhand or thumb knot which is the simplest true knot, sometimes used in sewing as a crude method of anchoring the end of the thread, and in rope as a strictly temporary means of preventing a rope's end from unravelling. It is liable to jam if pulled tight, and if not tightened it comes undone.

If the knot in fig. 8 is tightened round an object it is a half knot. This is the knot which the uninstructed usually makes when asked to make fast a rope, to the dismay of any seaman present who knows that as the start of a hitch this presages trouble. When tightened around an object of small diameter it tends to jam, and when not tightened, to capsize and become a half hitch (figs. 9 and 10). This capsizing action is deliberately induced when tying or untying a number of knots and is reversible.

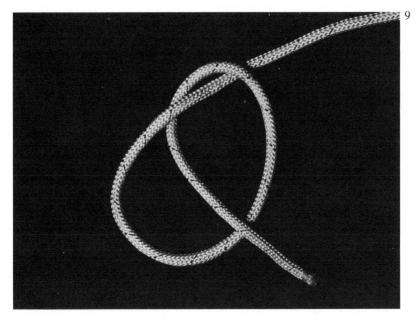

9

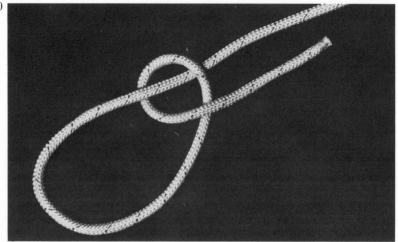

The half knot is a binding knot which is tied round an object or bundle of objects, usually with the two ends of a line, and depends for its security on the lateral pressure exerted upon it by the object round which it is tied. To prove this, first tie a half knot round a rolled magazine and then tie one round a book. The knot will bind on the convex surface of the magazine so that you can easily get it as tight as you wish, but the flat surface of the book exerts no lateral pressure against the knot and you will have difficulty in tightening it.

Having now made the acquaintance of all the basic formations from which any knot can be constructed we will list them and see how they are related to each other.

A loop is a drawn out bight.
A turn is a loop with its ends crossed.
A single hitch is a turn which incorporates nip.
A half hitch is a single hitch round its own standing part.
An overhand knot is a turn with the end tucked through it.
A half knot is an overhand knot that has been tied round something.

The last three can be converted from one into another without re-tying.

When a knot has to be made at some distance from the end of a line the seaman does not waste time in reeving the end and hauling several feet of rope through all the twists and turns of the knot, all of which would have to be repeated in reverse when he came to cast it off; he makes the knot 'on the bight' by doubling the working part into a loop which he uses as a new working end leaving the surplus line to become an idle part.

The bight is also used in three other ways, to make nooses, slip knots and slipped knots. A noose is a knot that has had a bight of the standing part drawn through it to form a loop which when placed round an object is progressively tightened by a strain on the standing part. The simplest form is the noose knot (fig. 11) when A is the standing part.

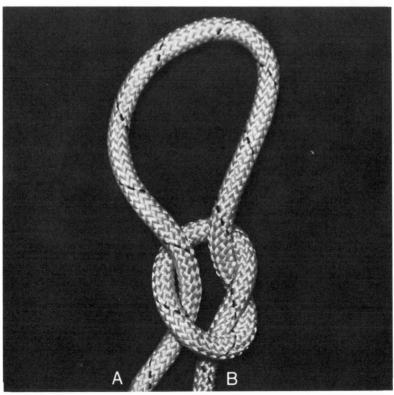

11

A   B

A slip knot is made entirely on the bight in such a way that a tug on the idle end causes the knot to spill completely. If the knot in fig. 11 is made with B as the standing part a pull on the working end A will cause the knot to disappear. The simplest practical form of slip knot is a single hitch which has been made by nipping a bight of the working end under the standing part. A slipped knot is one whose final stage is made with a bight of the working end so that when this is pulled the knot is partly spilled leaving at least a turn in place. The simplest example is the slipped half hitch, and perhaps the most familiar is the bow, which is a slipped reef knot.

The knots which we shall now examine are the recognisable descendants of the forms we have been discussing in this chapter. They are grouped in the order that best illustrates their construction rather than their function, but when you have learnt to tie a knot remember that unless you apply it to the correct use you have tied the wrong knot.

The knots described

1

Figure eight knot

This is a slight elaboration of the thumb knot in that the working end is taken round the standing part (fig. 2) before being stuck through the turn (fig. 3).

It is bulkier than the thumb knot and much easier to undo yet less apt to come undone when loosely formed. Used wherever a lump is needed in a rope, it is often seen in the ends of running gear to prevent a line from unreeving. When there is nothing better than a rock cleft to secure to, it can be used in the manner shown in fig. 4.

2

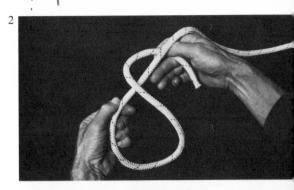

3

4

Figure eight loop

A strong and secure single loop knot suitable for use with a strain on either or both ends, and one of the few knots that is reliable in stiff or slippery material.

Pull out a bight of rope to form a loop and tie in the doubled rope exactly as the figure eight knot.

It suffers the disadvantages of using up a considerable length of rope and therefore being rather heavy and bulky, and of tightening under a heavy strain so that it can become difficult to undo; but it is so easily and quickly tied that anyone needing a loop knot in an emergency and being unsure of his ability to tie a bowline on a bight without hesitation would do well to make this knot instead.

Constrictor knot

Invented by Clifford Ashley, this binding knot consists of a single half knot clinched under one, two or three round turns.

To tie it put on the required number of round turns loosely over one end (fig. 1). Make a half knot with the two ends (fig. 2) and stick the other end back under the turns so that the two ends emerge on opposite sides (fig. 3). Take up the slack while ensuring that the turns lie parallel to one another and heave tight (fig. 4). The ends may then be trimmed flush.

Excellent as a temporary whipping on a rope's end or on individual strands while making multistrand knots and splicing. A series of constrictor knots can be used with advantage in place of a long seizing when repairing a spar because they are so much easier for the inexpert, or one working under difficulties, to get really tight. If the half knot is

5

slipped the knot makes a first
class bag closure.

In fig. 5 a constrictor has been
applied to a cut end to stop it
fraying while new whipping was
put on. The end can now be
fused by heat without damaging
the whipping.

1

Reef knot

Another good binding knot that lies flat and is easy to adjust, the reef knot owes its name to its use in tying up the parcel of idle material in a reefed sail: a use to which the ease and speed with which it can be tied and cast off admirably suit it.

It consists of two half knots reversed so that each is the mirror image of the other, with each end emerging alongside its own standing part. It is probably the first knot that most of us learn to tie.

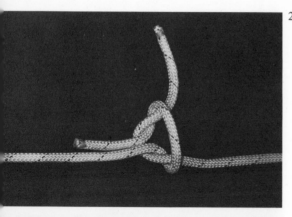

To cast off, grasp either end and give it a sharp tug in the direction of the other (figs. 2 and 3). This will capsize the knot into two reversed half hitches (fig. 4), that is to say a lark's head in one end round a straight end, which is equal to no knot at all and the two ends just fall apart (figs. 5 and 6).

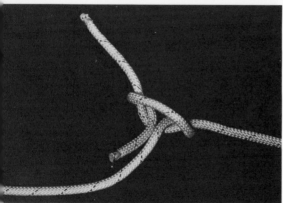

This reveals the knot's deadly weakness when used as a bend, for it can happen suddenly under strain, particularly if the two

ropes being joined differ in thickness, construction or material.

The reef knot should only be used as a binding knot, and for finishing the ends of seizings in twine. A good guide as to whether it is suitable for a particular job is the ease with which it can be tied tightly. On a convex surface like your instep or a rolled magazine there will be no difficulty in maintaining tension on the first overhand

knot while tying the second, but you will have the devil of a job on the flat surface of a parcel of books. So while it is fine for shoelaces and tying up well rounded objects it is wrong for tying up books or square boxes.

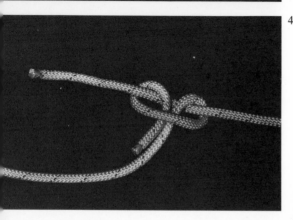

Here the knot is really acting as a bend, and will do so even more when some numbskull has picked up the parcel by the string and stretched it. For such a case it would be better to make a bowline in one end of the string and secure the other to it with a becket hitch.

The fallacy that a reef knot is suitable for joining two ropes of equal thickness has gained credence through constant reiteration. The fact is that the 'British Admiralty Manual of Seamanship' says that a reef knot *with the ends seized* can be used this way; but a reef knot is no more the equivalent of a reef knot and two seizings than a round turn is the equivalent of a round turn and two half hitches.

Now why should anyone bother with such a cumbersome and inefficient arrangement when there are plenty of better and simpler bends? The answer would seem to be that nearly all bends are rather bulky and their ends poke out at awkward angles, so they do not willingly pass fairleads in which they tend to snag and jam. But when it comes to passing a fairlead or going over a roller a reef knot with its ends seized is the next best thing to a chain, so it was adopted for the sake of this characteristic and everyone trusted to the seizings which were what really gave the knot security. In most circumstances it is possible to arrange the two joined lines so that the bend does not have to negotiate the fairlead, and then you can use a proper knot for the job, but if you really have to use a reef knot do not omit the seizings.

Finally if you ever need to

5

6

escape by climbing down a rope of knotted blankets, consider how easily you could initiate the sequence of events in figs. 2 to 6 and if you value your life do not use reef knots.

31

Granny and other disreputable relatives

None of these knots are fit for practical use so there will be no pictures, but you can have an interesting and instructive practical exercise in making their acquaintance and seeing how big small differences can be.

The granny as everyone knows is a reef knot gone wrong. It consists of two half knots made in the same direction instead of being reversed, so the ends come out sideways. The knot slips and may eventually jam.

When you have tied a granny, capsize it in the same manner as was used to cast off a reef knot and you will find that instead of a lark's head you have a regular two half hitches. Now withdraw the straightened end and pass it through the two half hitches from the opposite side, capsize it back into the reef knot/granny form and see what you get. Try the effect of pulling on first the working ends and then the standing ends and generally sniff out its characteristics.

Now do the same with the reef knot. You may think that this time the result is another reef knot because at first sight it looks the same, but it is not composed of two half knots and the ends do not emerge on the same side.

Surgeon's knot

In stiff or slippery material a reef
knot tends to work loose and this
close relative is more secure
though less easy to cast off. It is
made in a similar way to a reef
knot but each half knot is given
an extra turn (see above). When
subjected to heavy strain it takes
up an interesting shape and in
doing so gives slightly. In
modern materials it could well
supplant the reef knot in any
application that does not require
the latter's ease of release.

1

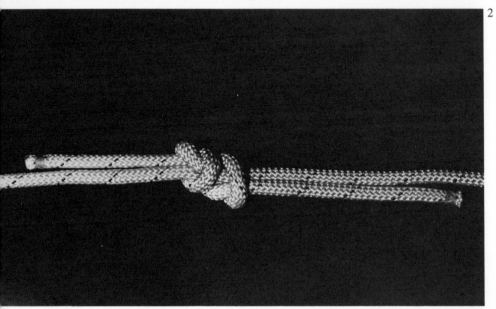

2

34

Englishman's knot

One of the simplest bends and secure if well snugged together before being subjected to strain, the Englishman's knot is made by tying a half knot in the end of each rope around the standing part of the other (figs. 1 and 2). Apart from its bulkiness which is a disadvantage inherent in most bends, the knot may become difficult to undo after being heavily loaded.

Anyone who uses knots infrequently and needs but few should include this one in his repertoire.

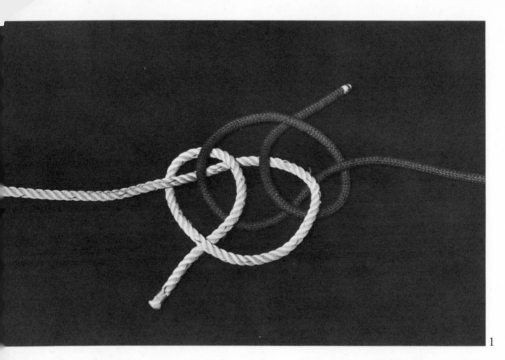

Hunter's bend

This beautiful knot also consists of two half knots but this time each interlocks twice with its neighbour (see above).

To tie, overlap the ends to be joined (fig. 2). Twist into a turn (fig. 3). Stick each end through the turn from the opposite side (figs. 4 and 5). Work tight carefully and the knot assumes the appearance of figs. 6 and 7 when viewed from opposite sides.

The easy nips of this knot are kind to the rope which make it a natural choice when very heavy loads are to be applied, and it can be used with ropes of different composition and thickness. It will neither slip nor jam and is always easy to cast off.

The truly extraordinary thing about this knot is that it is a recent invention. Ashley described a number of bends which are based on interlocking half knots and dismissed most of them as being unreliable or worse, but he overlooked this symmetrical arrangement which would surely have pleased his connoisseur's eye.

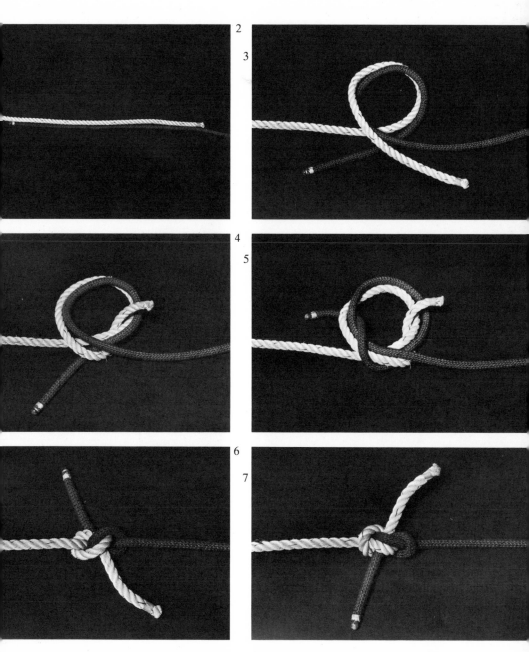

Carrick bend

The true carrick bend is a classic heavy duty bend which lends itself particularly well to being formed in the heaviest cables, the manipulation of which is a formidable task rendering impractical the formation of certain knots. Unfortunately, the name has been widely applied and won unmerited respectability for a whole series of unreliable or even dangerous impostors which are based on this pattern and that of the similar reef knot/granny series.

The one true carrick bend is shown here (fig. 1) opened out to display its construction which is symmetrical, of regular 'over and under' formation with the ends emerging on opposite diagonals, and under load (fig. 2) when it capsizes into a very different form.

No departure from this exact formation and no abbreviated so-called 'single carrick bend' is to be trusted. The sole defect of this excellent knot is the ease with which a disastrous mistake can be made in tying it.

1

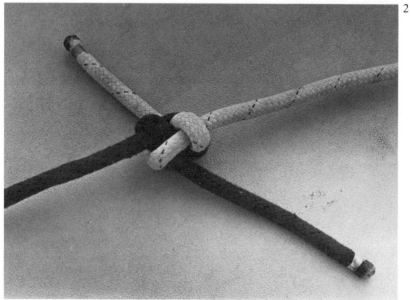

2

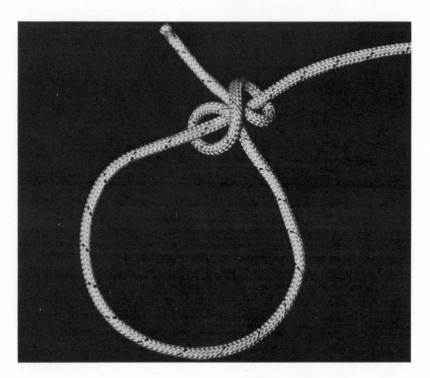

Two half hitches

One half hitch by itself is not a practical knot: like a loose nut on a bolt it will soon come undone, but a second half hitch acts as a lock-nut, taking hardly any of the strain yet ensuring that the first stays on the job. The half hitches should be made in the same direction (see above) and two of them are enough for anyone and any purpose; to use more is a sign of ignorance.

Not a very secure knot and prone to jam, this formation is chiefly used in conjunction with others in a range of important knots.

Buntline hitch

At first sight this looks exactly like the previous knot, but the two half hitches are put on in the reverse order so that the second is inside the first. This makes it extremely secure and it will stand up to any amount of shaking and jerking: it is less liable to jam than two half hitches, needing a greater strain to make it do so, but when pulled really tight it can become quite difficult to cast off. Unlike almost every other knot, the end of this one can safely be left very short so it is economical of material and light in weight.

Its lightness, freedom from chafe and imperviousness to flogging make it ideal for attaching sheets to small boat sails and light weather sails that do not impose heavy loads. It is the best knot for securing the end of a bucket lanyard; is good for tethering animals, and if slipped makes a secure halter hitch for a horse. Almost any knot that is normally finished off with two half hitches can be made more secure if the buntline hitch is substituted for the regular form.

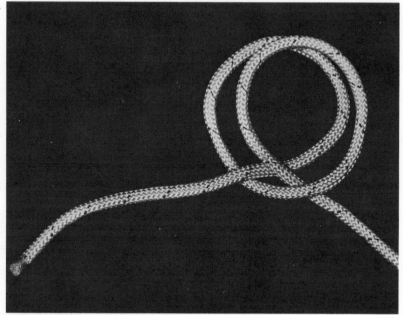

Clove hitch

This is the same formation as the two previous knots but made round another object instead of round its own standing part.

You would never guess from the profusion of clove hitches that bedizen yachts and fishing boats the world over that this is a specialised knot of limited usefulness. It is designed to take simultaneous loads on both ends from opposite directions and to grip the object to which it is secured. In the absence of these conditions some other knot would be better.

The classic application of the clove hitch at sea was to secure ratlines to the shrouds: it is still correctly employed in hitching a lifeline to a row of stanchions and in bending a flag halyard to a burgee stick.

When only one end is loaded it is insecure unless at least one additional half hitch is added round the standing part, and it will cast itself off completely if the object round which it is tied can rotate or if an animal tethered by it circles its picket continuously in one direction.

It can bind very tightly and become difficult to cast off, and is always awkward to cast off except when made on an open-ended object.

If it is to go over the end of a spar it can either be tied in hand

2
3
4
5

(figs. 2 to 6) or the two single hitches of which it is composed can be cast directly on. Either way the knack of twisting the rope to form the hitches is quickly learned.

6

43

Two half hitches reversed

This is the third of four possible arrangements of two half hitches. (The fourth being a vicious noose which jams, useful only to murderers, and in former days to shop assistants who were damned if you were going to get further use out of the parcel string.)

Lark's head or cow hitch

This hitch stands in the same relationship to two half hitches reversed as the clove hitch does to two half hitches. It too is used when there is a strain on both parts of the line but in the same direction.

It is the easiest of all hitches to make and cast off, and both operations can be performed with one hand. This makes it useful for hitching short lengths of line, tape and so on, to any convenient object for storage and instant retrieval.

To tie, middle the line (more than once if necessary to reduce it to a convenient length), pass the central loop round the object and draw the rest of it through the loop. For passing over an open-ended object it can be tied in hand even more easily than the clove hitch.

To cast off, grasp the central loop and pull. It does not bind and jam like the clove hitch.

2

Timber hitch

This is really a cross between a hitch and a binding knot, and like all such depends for its security on the lateral pressure exerted upon it by the object around which it is tied.

The working end is first taken round the standing part and then twisted, or *dogged,* round itself in the same direction as the lay of the rope (fig. 2).

The name comes from its use in hauling logs, but the ease with which this hitch can be made and cast off makes it particularly useful when a succession of objects has to be handled. Care must be taken to ensure that it is properly formed and settled round the load, and remains so whenever the strain comes off it.

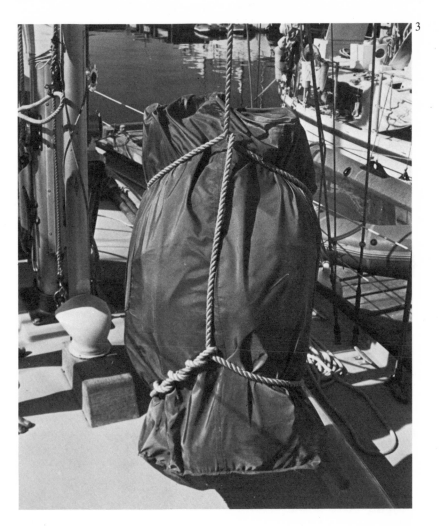

It is seen here (fig. 3) as often used with the standing part half hitched round the load to steady it.

    This knot also makes a quick and convenient method of securing the twine or marline at the start of a seizing.

Working end

Load

1 **Rolling hitch**
The purpose of the rolling hitch
is to attach a line to a spar or to
another line in such a way that it
will resist a lengthways pull
without slipping. The knot has a
ratchet action which allows it to
be slid one way but locks it
against a pull in the opposite
direction. It is secure and always
easy to cast off. There are two
versions depending on whether it
is to be attached to a spar or a
rope.

Supposing the direction of pull
to be downwards, put on a single
hitch with the working end
coming out below the standing
part (fig. 3) and take a plain turn
round the rope above it (figs. 4
and 5). Finish off with a second
single hitch on top (fig. 6). When
2 securing to a spar the middle turn
is taken below the single hitch
(fig. 2).

This is the knot to use when
you want to relieve the strain on
a rope in order to shift a lead or
clear a riding turn, but if the
strain is heavy the two ropes will
twist together: to prevent this
reverse the direction of the final
single hitch.

3

4

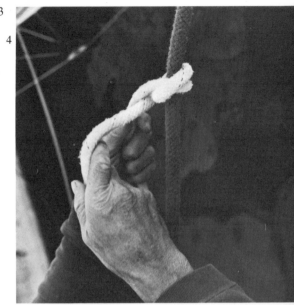

5

6

Midshipman's hitch

This is simply a rolling hitch taken with the tail of a rope round its own standing part to make an easily adjustable loop knot. It has a multitude of applications both at sea and ashore in jacklines, guy ropes, lashings, etc.

Idle end→

Standing part↓

1

Round turn and two half hitches

This is a very logical and seamanlike hitch, every element of its composition and every movement in its construction fulfilling a purpose. The round turn, which is very quickly cast on to a bollard or samson post, provides friction and allows the strain on the rope to be checked gently by surging; it prevents the inner half hitch from jamming and provides a good bearing surface to reduce chafe. There is less reason to use this knot when securing to a ring or rail but it is still a handy general purpose hitch and very easy to cast off. In modern materials its security is improved if the two half hitches are made in the form of a buntline hitch when it becomes a round turn and buntline hitch.

The sequence of pictures (figs. 2 to 6 overleaf) shows how it is made: the half hitches in this instance having been made 'on the bight'.

2

3

4

5

1

Fisherman's bend

The security of a round turn and two half hitches falls a little short of guaranteeing peace of mind in the long term, particularly when used out of sight or under water. The fisherman's bend is a slightly refined version in which the first half hitch is made through the round turn (figs. 2 and 3). This makes it much more secure at the cost of a little extra time in the making and casting off. Traditionally used to bend a rope cable to an anchor, which accounts for the name of this undoubted hitch, the end would be seized back to the standing part for additional security and to reduce the tendency of the inner half hitch to jam.

2

3

1

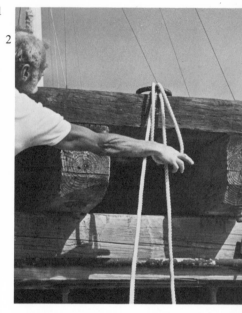

2

3

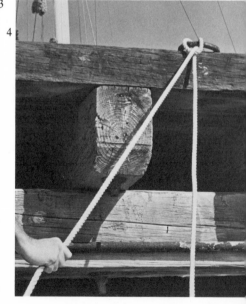

4

Backhanded hitch

When securing to an awkward or awkwardly sited object it is easier to pass a doubled line than a single end because the loop can be more easily retrieved. This hitch can be made with one hand.

Double several feet of the line back to form a long loop and pass it round or through the object (figs. 1 and 2).

Reach through the loop, grasp a bight of the working part and pull it through (figs. 3 and 4).

The hitch can be finished off with two half hitches, though in the circumstances in which this knot is typically used they may be rather inaccessible when you want to cast off, and a long bowline, which can be made at a point convenient to reach (fig. 5) would be more practical.

The combination of backhanded hitch and bowline enables you to make fast a towline to a car with a minimum of grovelling in the dirt, and also (since the rope is hauled back through its own bight and not round some greasy, gritty bit of the foul machine) without contaminating yards of good rope. The bowline should be tied clear of the vehicle altogether.

5

1

2

3

Standing part ← → Idle part

4

Draw hitch

When it is necessary to cast off and recover a line secured to an object that is difficult to reach, the most usual method is to rig a slip line round or through the object and secure both ends where you can reach them. When you want to cast off, you let go one end and recover the line by hauling on the other. Though perfectly secure the success of this operation may be jeopardised by an awkward lead causing too much friction or even a snag, or too great a length of line.

The draw hitch is a slip knot which clears its securing point instantaneously. Properly used it is secure in the short term but should not be left unattended. In careless hands it can be very dangerous.

To tie, make a loop on the bight long enough for the idle end to reach from the securing point back to the release point with plenty of slack. Pass the doubled line round or through the object (fig. 1), stick a bight of the standing part through this loop (fig. 2) and a bight of the idle part through the loop just formed (figs. 3 and 4). Draw snugly together and be careful to remember which end is which, so that the load is applied to the standing part only.

To release, give a sharp tug on the idle end and the knot will spill instantly (figs. 5 and 6).

5

6

1

Sheet bend, single and double

One of the simplest bends, widely used in the days of natural fibre ropes, it is prone to slip when tied in synthetic materials and in its single form is only suitable for light work. The double sheet bend is, however, reliable. Whether double or single there are two forms of this bend, the Right-handed in which the ends emerge on the same side, and the Left-handed whose ends emerge on opposite sides. Experiment has shown the Right-handed bend to be significantly more secure.

There are many different ways of tying this knot: landsmen who do not normally distinguish between the two forms usually make it in the form of a becket hitch. The method described here is not only the quickest and most seamanlike but ensures that the result is infallibly the right-hand version. After a little practice the knot can be tied in a single continuous movement.

Place the ropes to be joined alongside one another with their ends pointing in the same direction (fig. 2), and half knot them (fig. 3). Retain your grasp of the half knot and turn it so as to convert it into a single hitch with one rope around the other (fig. 4) (note that the ends are now pointing in opposite directions). While the left hand steadies the half hitch and with the right hand grasping the straightened end, pass it behind the standing part of the other rope (fig. 5) and stick it down through the half hitch so that it emerges alongside its own standing part (fig. 6).

To form a double sheet bend, which should be used for all

60

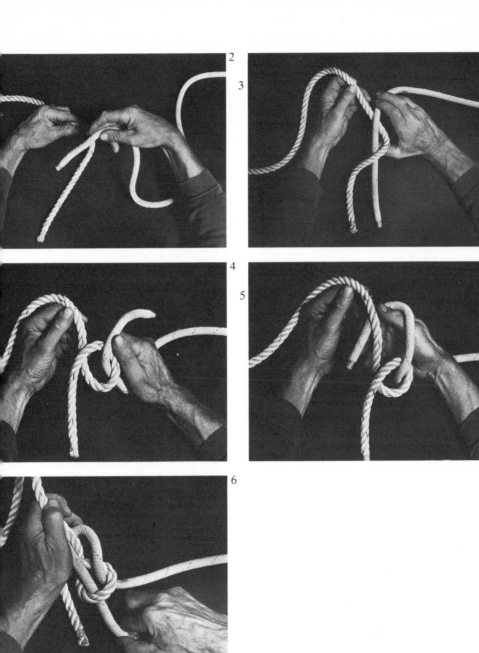

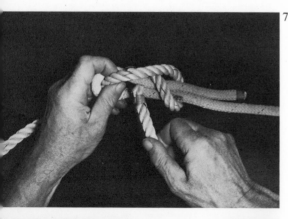

serious work, and always if the ropes being joined are not identical, first tie the single version and pass the half hitched end round once more following its own lead (figs. 7 and 8).

Tying a knot with short ends is unseamanlike: equivalent to using a bolt so short that only a couple of turns of thread are engaged by the nut: but it is sometimes unavoidable and justifiable, as when capturing a short protruding end, or a broken shoelace which usually turns out to be too short for its job if the repair uses more than a minimal amount of its length. The trick that follows has saved me an embarrassing delay on more than one occasion though a well organised person might go through life without ever having to use it, but useful or not, it is an illuminating experiment.

Make a noose knot as close to one end and as small as possible, remembering that the loop is made on the *standing part* (figs. 9 and 10), stick the short end through the noose (fig. 11) and then capsize the noose by pulling its end away from the standing part (fig. 12). The end to be joined will be drawn in (fig. 13) and turned round into a loop, and you will find the two ends united in a sheet bend (fig. 14).

As there is no easy way of ensuring that the result is a right and not a left-hand bend this method is not recommended as a regular way of making the knot.

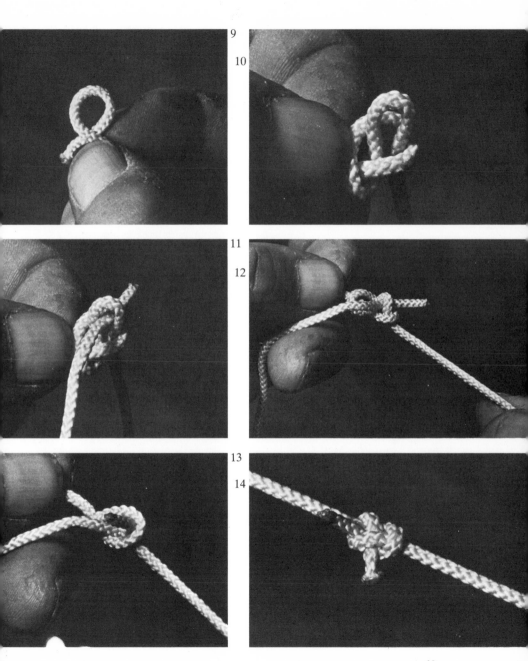

9
10
11
12
13
14

1

Becket hitch

This is identical in formation to the sheet bend but the plain loop end is replaced by an eye either of hardware or of rope. The difference between the two knots is that the becket hitch cannot be tied in the same way, and the distinction between right and left versions ceases to exist. The single working end is woven through the eye so as to reproduce the pattern of the sheet bend. Doubling the hitch is performed in a manner identical to doubling the sheet bend.

Fig. 1 shows a double becket hitch in use to attach a pair of headsail sheets.

To cast off a sheet bend or becket hitch that has pulled tight, bend it like this (figs. 2 and 3) and you will be able to work the turns loose.

Bowline

Everyone knows the bowline as a slip-proof loop knot, and sometimes it seems that everyone has a different way of tying it. I have chosen one method to demonstrate because it is the quickest; it can be applied just as the rope happens to lie without the need to rearrange it; there is no chance as there is with some methods of it resulting in an incorrect knot; the rope's end remains in the grasp of one hand from start to finish; it can be used in total darkness or underwater as easily as in any other circumstances.

Comparison of the bowline (fig. 1) with the sheet bend (page 60) shows that although they are totally different knots with totally different uses; one being a bend involving two separate ropes while the other is made with only one end in a single rope, their formation is identical and the hand movements made in tying them are precisely the same.

Begin by making a half knot but note that as only one rope is involved the working and standing ends point in opposite directions (fig. 2). Continue with the movements already

2

7   described for tying the right hand sheet bend (figs. 3 to 7), and after adjusting the loop to the required size carefully work the knot snug. The end will be found to lie parallel with and inside one leg of the loop.

The perceptive reader will realise that the alternative method of tying the sheet bend from a noose knot can be used to produce a bowline, and this is indeed true but it is a practice to be discouraged because as the briefest comparison of the two knots reveals, the bowline is only one of a number of loop knots that embody the sheet bend figure, and as these other knots range from inferior to worthless there is a grave risk in using a method devoid of any clear cut distinction between the one process that results in the correct knot and the slight variations that do not. Just how careful you need to be was brought home to me by a young woman whom I asked to tie a bowline. With great confidence and dexterity she flicked two turns into the rope, passed the end through one of them, gave a quick tug and triumphantly held out a loop knot which embodied the authentic sheet bend pattern. I had the utmost difficulty in convincing her that the knot she had made was not a bowline: she had been taught to tie a bowline by capsizing a noose, therefore the knot she had produced this way must be a bowline and I must be wrong. Unfortunately she had unknowingly got into the habit of making not a noose knot but a slip knot, which is all too easy when you consider that it had to be made at some distance from the ends of the rope where the distinction between standing and working parts is not all that obvious. More unfortunately her instructor had not warned her of this possibility.

Since it can be tied in hand and is resistant to slipping, the bowline is useful whenever a loop is needed to be got ready to pass over an object. It can also be made as long as you like and so enable you to secure to a relatively inaccessible object with a knot that can easily be reached for adjustment or release. It cannot be tied in a line that is under strain, and if made in stiff or slippery material and not kept under continuous strain, it tends to work loose; so it is a knot that calls for thoughtful use. Like most loop knots it is vulnerable to chafe and it may be advisable to incorporate a round turn in the loop.

8

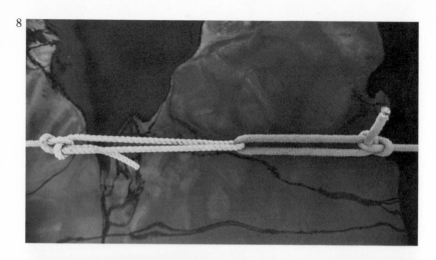

9

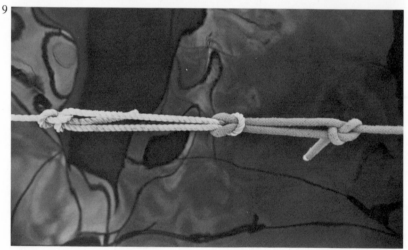

Two bowlines make a reliable bend (fig. 8) although in this arrangement the sharp nip is weakening and, if heavily loaded, chafe will be rapid. The nip can be eased and the chafe largely eliminated if the two ropes are loosely reef-knotted together before the bowlines are made (fig. 9). This in no way condones the use of the reef knot as a bend.

Running bowline

A noose made by tying a small bowline round the standing part may be used to improvise a crude, heavy but reliable lasso.

3

Bowline on a bight

If a bowline is needed with so much urgency that there is not time enough to free an end of rope, the nearest bight can be snatched up and a bowline put in it.

The knot is begun exactly as an ordinary bowline, using the doubled bight as if it were the end of the rope (figs. 1 and 2). Everything will naturally come out double including the loop. At the stage when in an ordinary bowline the end is passed round the standing part, instead open out the looped working end and pass it over the entire knot which is brought out through it in the manner of a garment being turned inside out (figs. 3 and 4). This causes the loop of the working end to encircle the two standing parts in the authentic bowline pattern (fig. 5) after which the loops are adjusted for size either independently or together and pulled tight (fig. 6).

4

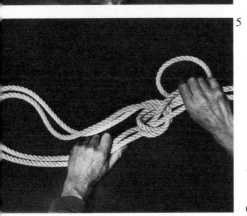

5

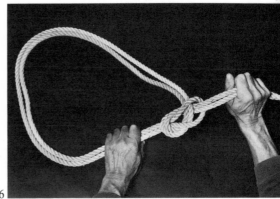

6

7

This knot has all the properties of the bowline and must be one of the most secure knots because it lacks a working end and cannot possibly come undone in use.

As everything is double it makes an admirable sling or bosun's chair (see opposite). It should be practised until it can be tied in an emergency without hesitation.

Glossary

becket: Permanent eye, either of hardware or rope.

bend: Knot which joins two ropes end to end.

bend, to:
1. To make a bend.
2. To secure sails to spars or rigging, or cable to an anchor.

bight:
1. Any slack part of rope between its ends.
2. A wide loop.

on the bight: A knot made with a part of the bight doubled to form a false working end.

bollard: Strong mooring point, usually cylindrical and either single or double.

bosun's chair: Seat or sling which a person sits in when going aloft.

capsize, to:
1. To turn upside down.
2. To alter the form of a knot without casting it off and without adding or subtracting anything.

cast off, to: To let go or untie a knot.

dog, to:
1. to twist a rope's end several times round another part with the lay of the rope.
2. To make a series of spaced out single hitches with one rope round another one or chain.

eye:	A closed loop in rope or in hardware.
fairlead:	Guide to ensure that a rope or chain follows the required path. (In the USA CHOCK.)
gasket:	Short length of cordage or banding used to secure furled sails.
hitch:	Knot joining a rope to another object, to the bight of another rope, or to an eye or loop in the end of a rope.
in hand:	A knot is said to be tied 'in hand' when it is made round nothing but air.
knot:	1. Loose term to cover any organisation of cordage involving nip. 2. Lump, knot or loop in cordage as distinct from a bend or hitch.
lay:	Direction of twist in a rope's construction.
with the lay:	Conforming to the lay.
lead:	Direction taken up by a rope.
lead, to:	To organise a rope so that it follows the required lead.
loop:	A bight drawn out narrow but not crossed.
loop knot:	Knot forming a fixed eye.
running loop:	Loop knot tied round its own standing part to form a noose.
middle, to:	To double a line at its centre and so halve its length.
nip:	Point of pressure and friction at the crossing of two points of rope or at a sharp change of direction in rope round another object.

nip, to:	To create nip by any means.
noose:	Knot incorporating a loop at the standing part which draws up tight under strain.
ratlines:	Rungs of light line or batten for climbing the standing rigging.
reeve, to:	Pass the end of a line through an opening.
rove:	Past tense of reeve.
running part:	Part of line or tackle that runs, as distinct from the standing part.
running rigging:	Rigging used for hoisting and hauling and therefore having no more than one end permanently secured.
seizing:	Lashing consisting of numerous tight turns of twine or small stuff.
shroud:	Lateral or 'athwartships' member of the standing rigging.
slip line:	Line passed through or round an object and having the running part led back and secured adjacent to the standing part so that it can be cast off and recovered.
slip knot:	Knot designed to spill and let go completely when triggered by a tug on the idle end.
slipped knot:	Knot that comes partly undone when triggered.
small stuff:	Light cordage less than 8mm diameter, twine, marline, etc.
stanchion:	Vertical post, pillar or similar support.
standing end:	Fixed end of a line.

standing part:	1. Part of line adjacent to the standing end. 2. Part of line inactive in the making of a knot.
standing rigging:	Rigging which is permanently secured at both ends.
surge, to:	Take up or ease off strain on a line by allowing it to render round an object.
turn:	Formation of line capable of encircling an object once.
round turn:	Two turns (two round turns = three turns).
working end/part:	Part of line active in knot making.